Mike and Gordie

An Easy Guide to Bigfoot

D1096949

Written by Jerry Carino
Illustrated by Alla Mart

"Every single country has its version. Yeti, Yowie in Australia, Wild Man in China. So I don't know if it's perhaps a myth that stems from maybe the last of the Neanderthals. But then is the last of the Neanderthals still living in these remote forests? I don't know. But I'm not going to say it doesn't exist..."

Jane Goodall

Introduction

The idea to make a comic strip about Mike and Gordie came to me in a flash. Why wouldn't people want to read a comic strip about a teenage boy and a young, friendly Bigfoot who moved in next door?   It was obvious to me that this teenager (Mike) and this Bigfoot (Gordie) would become close, learn from each other and teach us a few life lessons along the way!

Many of the comic strips will contain some reference to Bigfoot lore. To me and to any hardcore Bigfoot enthusiast, they are usually obvious, but to those who are naive to the legend of Bigfoot, they might require some explanation. For many of the strips there will be some basic information and discussion about Bigfoot based on the most generally accepted "facts." I'm sure some will disagree with these facts, my writings and opinions, but that is part of the fun of Bigfoot!

Welcome to the world of Mike and Gordie. I hope that you enjoy their adventures and are able to learn a little bit more about both Bigfoot and friendship!

Chapter 1:

MIKE MEETS GORDIE

The Silhouette

The Bigfoot Silhouette is the most famous depiction of Bigfoot and can be found all over the internet, on t-shirts, mugs and many other products that want to use Bigfoot to sell things. There are often slight variations, but when you see one, it's unmistakable. It's based on the profile of the Bigfoot seen in the famous Patterson-Gimlin film from 1967 (more on that later!!)

Bigfoot is a master of disguise

As everyone knows, Bigfoot is a master of hiding in the woods. He can be right in front of you and you wouldn't even know it unless he wanted you to see him!

I think that he's just a savvy animal who knows how to hide. I mean, when's the last time you saw a bear or a moose or a cougar, but you know they are there! Some crazier theories say that he lives in another dimension and just shows up when he wants to or that you can't see him because of his "magic hypnosis powers." But I don't believe that.

MIKE AND GORDIE

OH MIKE, DON'T BE RIDICULOUS. THERE IS NO BIGFOOT OUTSIDE YOUR WINDOW!

HE WAS THERE! I SAW HIM!

OH, JUST RELAX! THERE IS NOTHING OUT THERE.

THUD!

AAAAAAAH!

© 2021 G. CARINO

Knocks

Bigfoots are really quiet animals and masters of hiding in the woods. But they are not silent! A common sound that they make is the "knock" or an occasional thud in the woods. Bigfoot explorers will often make a loud knocking sound in the forest by banging two pieces of wood together or a large branch against a tree. Then they wait for a wood knock response from Bigfoot...

MIKE AND GORDIE

I'VE GOT TO GO OUTSIDE AND LOOK!

WHOA!

Footprints

The most well known and iconic proof for Bigfoot being a real, undiscovered primate is the large footprints that people often find and report. Plaster casts are made, kept and displayed as evidence. Some of the casts have been up to 24 inches in length!

True believers focus on the dermal ridges and even scars that are often found on the casts and point out that they are almost impossible to fake. Skeptics point to casts that are obviously not authentic and use them to debunk the whole theory.

The British explorer David Thompson is sometimes credited with the first discovery (1811) of a set of Sasquatch footprints, and hundreds of alleged prints have been found since then. Dr. Jeff Meldrum is a Full Professor of Anatomy & Anthropology at Idaho State University who teaches human anatomy classes. His lab has more than 300 Bigfoot footprints which he studies and points to as proof of Bigfoot's existence.

MIKE AND GORDIE

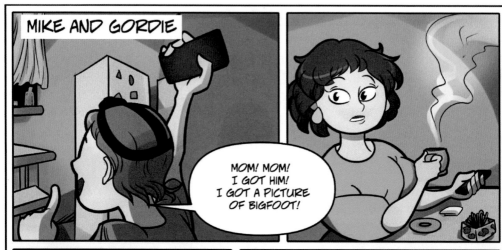

MOM! MOM! I GOT HIM! I GOT A PICTURE OF BIGFOOT!

OK, LET ME SEE.

HOW DID THAT HAPPEN!? HE WAS RIGHT THERE!

I DON'T SEE ANYTHING. JUST GET READY FOR SCHOOL.

Pictures of Bigfoot

Somehow, almost every picture of Bigfoot ever taken has been really blurry or he's been hiding behind a tree. Now almost everyone has a powerful camera in their phones, so it's just a matter of time until we get a clear close-up!

MIKE AND GORDIE

MIKE, I'M NOT SURE WHAT YOU SAW, BUT YOU'D BETTER HURRY UP, YOU'LL MISS THE BUS.

DING DONG!

HI! I'M GORDIE!

Encountering Bigfoot

If you should stumble upon a Bigfoot while you're out in the forest, most people would recommend you to be cautious. No one really knows how the Bigfoot would respond, and he or she would clearly be stronger and faster than you!

Many people believe they'd calmly stick around to take pictures or get proof of the encounter, but in reality most people would likely be terrified and have an instinct to run. If you do spot Bigfoot, remain calm, don't get in its way and just let it be. It's not the kind of creature you want to challenge in the wild! It is important to note that there are no modern reports of humans being harmed or killed by Bigfoot, so many people think they are not dangerous to people. You are probably safe.

Chapter 2:

MIKE AND GORDIE RIDE THE BUS

MIKE AND GORDIE

© 2021 G CARINO

Bigfoot vs Sasquatch

Bigfoot and Sasquatch are basically different names for the same thing.

The word "Sasquatch" is thought to come from the Salish Peoples of the Pacific Northwest of the US. Their word "se'sxac" means "wild men" and has been used to describe the hairy, ape-like creature that is sometimes discussed in their history and folklore.

The term "Bigfoot" was first coined by a journalist in Humboldt County, California named Andrew Genzoli in 1958 when writing about some footprints discovered in the woods. He originally use the term "Big Foot" but then changed it to one word. The article caught on nationally and interest in Bigfoot really grew from there.

Early Records of Bigfoot

Five hundred to 1000 year-old rock carvings on the Tule River Indian Reservation at a site called Painted Rock show a group of individuals called "the Family." Some people say that this is a group of Bigfoot and the local people call the largest image the "Hairy Man."

The Lummi people of the Pacific Northwest tell many stories of what they called the *Ts'emekwe* and the Iroquois of the Northeast talk about the *Genoskwa* or "Stone Giant." In some versions, the creature is very aggressive and violent, however in others he is very peaceful and is even able to communicate with the native peoples.

In 1929, J.W. Burns, an agent for the U.S. Bureau of Indian Affairs published a collection of local stories called "Introducing B.C.'s Hairy Giants" in a British Columbia newspaper. In it, he documented experiences from a number of the Sts'Ailes Peoples and utilized the term "Sasquatch."

The "Bigfoot Capital of the World"

Willow Creek, California is the self-declared "Bigfoot Capital of the World" located in Humboldt County, northern California. The town is easily reached by following California State Route 96, also known as the "Bigfoot Scenic Highway."

When in town, you can visit the Bigfoot Museum, attend the annual "Bigfoot Daze" festival (usually in September) or hike along Bluff Creek where many Bigfoot sightings have been made. In fact, the Patterson-Gimlin film was filmed along Bluff Creek about 50 miles outside of town!

© 2021 G CARINO

Bigfoot Believers

There are a large number of Bigfoot believers all around the world. Bigfoot appears regularly in popular culture and there are several organizations that are dedicated to investigating Bigfoot sightings.   One of the oldest and largest is the Bigfoot Field Researchers Organization (BFRO). Their website describes reports from all around North America and includes many instances of what they think are true Bigfoot.   However, they do describe and debunk some hoaxes as well.

A number of private researchers and groups own and operate Bigfoot museums. A quick search of the internet shows that there are museums in Willow Creek, California, West Virginia, Nebraska, Oregon and other locations. Bigfoot conferences and festivals are regularly attended by thousands of people!

MIKE AND GORDIE

GREAT, I'VE NEVER BEEN ON A BUS BEFORE EITHER!

THIS IS BILL, OUR BUS DRIVER.

HI BILL, I'M GORDIE!

WOOP! WOOP!

HEY GORDIE, SIT DOWN AND CLOSE THAT WINDOW!!!

© 2021 G CARINO

Bigfoot Vocalizations:

Bigfoot eyewitnesses report many sounds coming from Bigfoot. They describe hearing howls, woops, growls, screams, mumbles, whistles and other strange sounds in the woods and attribute them to Bigfoot. Some people even argue that Bigfoot can understand human languages, use sticks and rocks to communicate in a form of written language or even communicate telepathically!

Between 1972-1975, Ronald Morehead and Alan Berry recorded more than 90 minutes of sounds in the Sierra Nevada Mountains that they attribute to Bigfoot (the "Sierra Sounds"). They never saw Bigfoot, but they heard him. A retired Naval codebreaker named R. Scott Nelson has studied the Sierra Sounds and thinks they are definitely a language, are not human and could not have been faked. He now believes that he can speak Bigfoot and has even created a Sasquatch Phonetic Alphabet (SPA) to help understand it!

Patterson-Gimlin Film

Wow, I can write a lot about this! This is the most famous video ever of Bigfoot and was filmed in 1967 by Roger Patterson and Robert Gimlin in Humboldt County, (northern) California. The film is 53 seconds long and shows a big furry creature walking on 2 legs across a creek with a funny gait and giving a nice look towards the camera. I'm sure you've seen it and if you haven't, look it up online.

Patterson and Gimlin were in town filming a documentary about, yes, Bigfoot when they saw him. They were the only witnesses and Patterson claimed it was authentic til the day he died a few years later in 1973. Bob Gimlin claims he was not involved in a hoax, but stated that he guesses he could have been tricked by Roger Patterson. Over the years, many people have discredited the film, including a costume maker who claims to have sold Patterson the suit just a few months before the video was filmed (more about this later.)

The gait of the Bigfoot in the film is most often used as support for its authenticity. Believers, including some scientists, state that the gait can't be replicated by a human. Gait researchers (that's a real thing!) from Stanford tried to do so and were unable to fully copy it.

Chapter 3:

MIKE AND GORDIE IN SCHOOL

MIKE AND GORDIE

JAMES ALLISON?

HERE!

ELLA MILLER?

HERE!

GORDON RIVERS? GORDON?

I'M GORDIE!

MIKE AND GORDIE

SO GORDIE, YOU'RE NEW HERE. CAN YOU TELL US ABOUT YOURSELF?

WELL, I JUST MOVED HERE WITH MY DAD.

WE CAME FROM NORTHERN CALIFORNIA.

BUT WE'VE BEEN IN WASHINGTON, TEXAS, PENNSYLVANIA AND EVEN OKLAHOMA.

WOW, YOU'VE LIVED IN A LOT OF PLACES!

YEAH, WE REALLY GET AROUND!

Most Popular Places for Bigfoot Sightings

In 2019, the Travel Channel listed the top 8 states in the U.S. with the most Bigfoot sightings (some may surprise you!) They were:
1. Washington
2. California
3. Pennsylvania
4. Michigan
5. New York
6. Ohio
7. Oregon
8. Texas

West Virginia, Idaho and Montana have a lot per capita! Rhode Island (where I live) has very little.

Lawmakers in Oklahoma have actually introduced a Bigfoot Hunting Season for 2021. At least it's just for trapping, not shooting!!

MIKE AND GORDIE

HEY GORDIE, COME SIT WITH US!

SORRY GUYS, I'M GOING TO SIT WITH MIKE.

MIKE AND GORDIE

OH THIS IS MY FAVORITE! CHICKEN FINGERS!

GORDIE, WHY DON'T YOU TRY SOME?

NO, THANKS. I'M A VEGETARIAN

© 2021 G CARNO

What does Bigfoot eat?

No one really knows what Bigfoot eats. Many of our human ancestors and current primates follow a primarily vegetarian diet. Gorillas, for example, eat mostly shoots, stems and fruit but have developed a taste for termites and ants. Chimpanzees also eat mostly fruit, seeds and insects, but follow a more omnivorous diet as they will hunt other wildlife like small monkeys and deer for meat.

Bigfoot have been described to eat fruit very commonly and this is often used to lure them into camera traps (with little success). There is an abundance of wildlife (like deer and fish) in common Bigfoot habitat and many Bigfoot researchers claim that Bigfoot hunts and does eat meat.

But I'd like to think that Bigfoot is a vegetarian.

Chapter 4:

MIKE AND GORDIE PLAY BASKETBALL

MIKE AND GORDIE

OH, I'M NOT GOOD AT BASKETBALL. NO ONE EVER PICKS ME

LET'S PICK SIDES. GORDIE, WHO DO YOU WANT?

I'LL TAKE MIKE!

OK, IT'S ME AND JACK, VERSUS MIKE AND GORDIE!

MIKE AND GORDIE

SEE, I TOLD YOU I'M NOT GOOD. YOU SHOULDN'T HAVE PICKED ME.

OF COURSE I PICKED YOU! YOU ARE GOING TO WIN THE GAME FOR US!

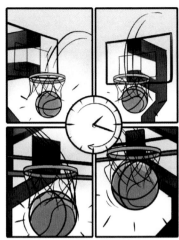

OK, THE GAME IS TIED. NEXT SHOT WINS, I WILL GIVE IT TO YOU TO TAKE IT!

GREAT SHOT, MIKE!

MIKE AND GORDIE

WOW! I'VE NEVER WON A GAME LIKE THAT! HOW DID YOU KNOW I'D MAKE IT?

I DIDN'T KNOW YOU'D MAKE IT, BUT I BELIEVE IN YOU!

YOU BELIEVE IN ME?

YES, I BELIEVE IN YOU! YOU SHOULD BELIEVE IN YOURSELF!

THANKS GORDIE, LET'S PLAY!

Evidence vs. Proof

There is a big difference between evidence and proof. Evidence is data or facts that lead us to try to prove the existence of something. Right now, there is a lot of evidence that suggests that there is a large, bipedal, hairy, ape-like creature wandering around the backwoods of the United States and Canada. All the pictures and videos, footprint casts, sounds and even nests and other signs can all be considered evidence. DNA evidence of hair samples showing an identified primate DNA would be particularly strong evidence and a number of scientists are trying to do just that.

Strong evidence could lead to a final conclusion of proof. At this point the evidence for Bigfoot to prove his existence is enough for some people, but not quite enough for most. Stronger evidence, like an actual captured Bigfoot or dead Bigfoot, would lead to proof.

Chapter 5:

MIKE BACK AT HOME

MIKE AND GORDIE

MOM! MOM! GORDIE IS SO COOL!

THAT'S GREAT, MIKE! SO GLAD THAT YOU'RE MAKING A FRIEND. YOU DON'T HAVE TOO MANY...

I KNOW. GORDIE IS AWESOME, JUST MOVED HERE WITH HIS DAD.

WHAT ABOUT HIS MOM?

OH, THERE IS NO MOM HERE. IT'S JUST THE TWO OF THEM.

HMMM, INTERESTING...

Bigfoot Family Tree

It's really unclear if Bigfoot are solitary or if they live in family units. A number of sightings have been reported of what appears to be a fully-grown Bigfoot with or even holding a baby or smaller Bigfoot.

Some Bigfoot believers think that Bigfoot could be a surviving population of *Gigantopithecus*. *Gigantopithecus* was a type of large, gorilla-like ape that lived in Asia and is thought to have gone extinct 300,000 years ago. Only teeth and jaw fossils have been found, so it's unclear how large they were or if they were bipedal, but many estimates put them at 400-600 pounds. Many fossils have been found in Asia, but none in North America.

MIKE AND GORDIE

MIKE, YOU'VE GOT TO INTRODUCE ME TO GORDIE'S DAD.

I WONDER WHAT HE'S LIKE...

MOM!

OH, THERE HE GOES!

© 2021 G CARINO

Chapter 6:

MIKE AND GORDIE OUTSIDE

MIKE AND GORDIE

LETS PLAY HIDE AND SEEK!

YOU DON'T WANT TO PLAY HIDE AND SEEK WITH ME. I'M TOO GOOD AT IT!

THAT SOUNDS LIKE A CHALLENGE! I'LL FIND YOU, GORDIE!

...7,8,9. READY OR NOT! HERE I COME!

GOTCHA MIKE!

A FEW HOURS LATER...

GORDIE, GORDIE! WHERE ARE YOU?

© 2021 G CARINO

As we discussed earlier, Bigfoot is almost impossible to find if he doesn't want to be seen. Some have even called him the "Hide and Seek World Champion!"

MIKE AND GORDIE

OK EVERYONE, HERE I AM!

LET'S PLAY AGAIN. I'LL TAKE IT EASY THIS TIME!

...7,8,9. READY OR NOT! HERE I COME!

OH MY GOSH, WHAT'S THAT SMELL?!?

OH SORRY, THAT'S MY UNCLE DARRYL! HE'S VISITING FROM FLORIDA.

© 2021 G CARINO

The Skunk Ape

There are a large number of animals similar to Bigfoot that are described all over the world. The Skunk Ape is found in the southeastern U.S. (mostly in Florida) and, as the name suggests, has a horrible smell. Reports of the skunk ape were really common from the 1950's to 1970's leading to a failed attempt to pass a bill in the state legislature in 1977 making it illegal "take, possess, harm or molest anthropoids or humanoid animals" in the state of Florida. So, I guess those things are still legal in Florida.

In 2000, a famous picture known as the "Myakka Skunk Ape" was anonymously sent to the Sarasota Sheriff's office showing a large, hairy ape-like creature that the author said was stealing fruit from her backyard. Some people think that it is the best picture ever of a large, undescribed primate, the skunk ape. The picture is pretty scary and doesn't really look like any known ape suits or primates.

Chapter 7:

MIKE AND GORDIE GO CAMPING

MIKE AND GORDIE

THANKS FOR TAKING ME CAMPING, I'VE NEVER DONE IT BEFORE.

YEAH, IT'S SO GREAT TO GET SOME FRESH AIR!

WOW! DID YOU SEE THAT!? THAT WAS A UFO!

COME ON, GORDIE. YOU DON'T BELIEVE IN ALIENS, DO YOU?

OF COURSE I DO, MIKE! WE ARE NOT ALONE!

Bigfoot as Aliens?

Some Bigfoot investigators think that it's possible that Bigfoot are actually alien lifeforms on this planet.   But that's a lot.

MIKE AND GORDIE

Other Cryptids

Cryptozoologists study <u>cryptids</u>: animals or creatures whose existence has yet to be proven. Bigfoot is probably the most famous cryptid, at least in North America. The Loch Ness Monster ("Nessie"), the Jersey Devil, El Chupacabra and Mothman, are other commonly discussed crytpids. The International Crytpotozoology Museum in Portland, ME is a great museum with an awesome Bigfoot section.

As you think about crytpids, it's important to note that some *real* species were once considered cryptids before they were definitively discovered. These include the komodo dragon, the platypus, the giant squid and even gorillas!

MIKE AND GORDIE

WHY DID YOU LET HIM GO? I'M HUNGRY FOR BREAKFAST!

OH, YOU KNOW, I DON'T EAT MEAT. ANYWAY, I'LL FIND US FOOD!

TRY THESE, THESE ARE GREAT!

YUM. LET'S FIND SOME MORE!

READY TO EAT!

MIKE AND GORDIE

CRACK!

OH, IT'S JUST YOUR DAD!

THAT'S NOT MY DAD, THAT'S A BEAR!

STAY STILL, PERFECTLY STILL! HE WILL GO AWAY.

WHEW!

Misidentification of Bigfoot

Black bears are likely the animal most often mistakenly identified as Bigfoot. Bears have been seen to walk upright on 2 legs, at least for short periods of time, and this could contribute to the misidentification. Black bears are 5-7 feet tall when standing upright while grizzly bears can be 8-9 ft tall.

In 2007, the Bigfoot Field Researchers Organization put out a photograph from Pennsylvania of an animal with patchy fur that they claimed to be a young Bigfoot. It received a lot of attention. The state game commission stated that it was just a bear with mange.

Many humans have also been mistaken for Bigfoot. There are a number of stories where hunters have even mistakenly shot other people that they thought were Bigfoot.

Chapter 8:

MIKE AND GORDIE IN THE SNOW

MIKE AND GORDIE

YEAH! SNOW!

THEY JUST ANNOUNCED NO SCHOOL TODAY.

HEY GORDIE, LET'S GO OUTSIDE AND MAKE A SNOWMAN!

CAN'T WAIT TO GET GORDIE WITH A SNOWBALL!

GORDIE? GORDIE?

WHAM!

HA HA HA!

© 2021 G CARINO

Bigfoot's Speed

Thousands of Bigfoot sightings have occurred over the years. In a very small number of sightings, Bigfoot was noted to be running alongside a car or vehicle. In those special sightings, we are able to get an estimate of Bigfoot's running speed. A cluster of sightings seem to put the top running speed at 35-40 mph, which is about as fast as a grizzly bear or a greyhound!! Some sightings at 60+ mph were probably hoaxes or errors in measurement.

Walking speed is also quite fast, estimated at 10 mph, which is much faster than the average human walking speed of 3-4 mph. They have also been reported to have a 6-8 foot vertical leap and 14-22 foot horizontal leap which would allow them to jump across an entire road very easily.

MIKE AND GORDIE

LET'S MAKE A SNOWMAN!

TAH-DAH!

WOW, THAT'S AWESOME!

YOURS IS REALLY AMAZING, TOO!

Other Bigfoot relatives

The yeti, of course, is another "Bigfoot-like" creature and is from the Himalaya Mountains of Asia. It is also commonly referred to as the Abominable Snowman. This term was first coined in 1921 when British Lieutenant-Colonel Charles Howard-Bury, while exploring Nepal and Mt. Everest, noted and photographed some large footprints in the snow. His Sherpa guides suggested that they came from the "'metoh-kangmi'" which translated to the man-bear snowman.

The yeti does have a long history in Sherpa folklore, but many to think that they are just misidentified bears or yaks. In 2013 an Oxford professor, Bryan Sykes conducted DNA analysis on some hair samples that were reported to be from a yeti sighting. One of the samples appeared to come from a hybrid of brown bear and polar bear which is not known to exist in the Himalayas. This gave some support to the theory that there is an unidentified animal there that may just be the yeti. Unfortunately, follow-up studies on the samples just came up with brown bear as the likely source.

Other less common similar creatures are the alma (or almasty) of Central Asia, the yeren of China, the yowie from the Australian outback and the orang pendek of Indonesia. The orang pendek is most often described as much shorter than Bigfoot (3-5 feet tall), but all the others are similarly described as tall, hairy "wild men."

MIKE AND GORDIE

MADE YOU HOT CHOCOLATE, TAKE OFF YOUR BOOTS AND COATS.

MY ZIPPER'S STUCK

© 2021 G. CARINO

Bigfoot Hoaxes

Many of the reported Bigfoot sightings are just hoaxes. A number of hoaxes have been uncovered in which Bigfoot was just a man in a gorilla suit or even military ghillie suit. Some hoaxes have been simple and others really elaborate.

Many people think that the most famous evidence for Bigfoot, the 1967 Patterson-Gimlin film, was just an elaborate hoax. Roger Patterson died in 1973 and always insisted that the video was real. However, in the 1980's, Phillip Morris who owned a Hollywood costume shop came forward saying that Roger Patterson had ordered a gorilla suit from him just a few months before the film. He even states that Patterson asked him how to make the person under the suit look bigger, how to extend the arms and even how to hide the zipper!

Morris said he knew right away that it was his suit in the film, but expected Patterson to "come clean" after a few weeks. Years after Patterson died, he decided that it was OK to tell people.

Chapter 9:

MIKE AND GORDIE PLAY BASEBALL

MIKE AND GORDIE

COME ON GORDIE, GET A HIT!

Ball!

Ball!

Ball!

Ball Four!

Walk!

© 2021 G CARIN

MIKE AND GORDIE

STEAL! STEAL!!

GREAT JOB GORDIE! JUST NEED ONE MORE RUN TO WIN!

MIKE AND GORDIE

THERE'S GONNA BE A PLAY AT THE PLATE! SLIDE!

SAFE!

OH NO! HE WAS OUT!

LETS GO TO THE VIDEO REPLAY.

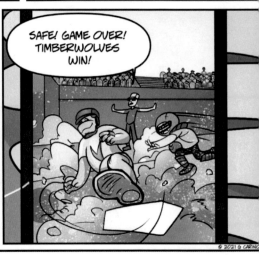

SAFE! GAME OVER! TIMBERWOLVES WIN!

Chapter 10:

SCHOOL'S OUT FOR MIKE AND GORDIE

MIKE AND GORDIE

WOW, I CAN'T BELIEVE THAT THE SCHOOL YEAR IS ALMOST OVER!

YEAH, IT'S BEEN A REALLY FUN YEAR.

GORDIE, DID YOU GET A YEARBOOK? CAN YOU SIGN MINE?

ABSOLUTELY, AS LONG AS YOU SIGN MINE!

BRRINNNNG!!!

OOPS, GOTTA GET TO CLASS!

MIKE AND GORDIE

HEY MOM, CHECK IT OUT, WE GOT OUR YEARBOOKS TODAY!

MARCHING BAND

THE PROM

THAT'S GREAT, DID GORDIE SIGN IT FOR YOU?

YES! LET'S CHECK IT OUT!

© 2021 G CARINO

Final Word

There are believers in Bigfoot and probably many more non-believers. I'm not sure if Bigfoot exists, but I certainly hope that he does.

When and if we finally ever come face to face with Bigfoot and we prove him a true animal and not a cryptid, it would be an amazing event. Hopefully our interactions will be peaceful and we treat him with well-deserved respect. We will surely be able to learn from one another, just like Mike and Gordie did!

ABOUT THE AUTHOR:

erry Carino is a practicing pulmonary and critical care doctor who has always
een interested in cryptozoology. He has published multiple times in the
ıedical fields, but this is his first work that he has done just for fun. He lives
ı Pawtucket, Rhode Island with his wife and 2 children. Contact me at
ıikeandgordie@gmail.com.

ABOUT THE ARTIST:

la Mart is a young digital artist from Kharkiv, Ukraine, specializing in funny
ɔmic strips. Making humorous stories is her passion.

Made in the USA
Las Vegas, NV
27 February 2022

44679473R00050